D0952449

Cambridge English Readers

....

Level 4

Series editor: Philip Prowse

The Lady in White

Colin Campbell

CAMBRIDGE
UNIVERSITY PRESS

PUBLISHED BY THE PRESS SYNDICATE OF THE UNIVERSITY OF CAMBRIDGE
The Pitt Building, Trumpington Street, Cambridge, United Kingdom

CAMBRIDGE UNIVERSITY PRESS
The Edinburgh Building, Cambridge CB2 2RU, UK
40 West 20th Street, New York, NY 10011-4211, USA
477 Williamstown Road, Port Melbourne, VIC 3207, Australia
Ruiz de Alarcón 13, 28014 Madrid, Spain
Dock House, The Waterfront, Cape Town 8001, South Africa

http://www.cambridge.org

First published 1999
Seventh printing 2005

Printed in India by Thomson Press (India) Limited

Typeset in 12/15pt Adobe Garamond [CE]

ISBN 0 521 66620 1

Contents

Characters

John: a successful television producer.
Jenny: John's assistant.
Rachel: John's wife.
Patrick: the young son of Rachel and John.
Mrs Reagan: the woman from the pub on Inishbofin.
A policeman.
The man who gives the hitch-hiker a lift.
The lady in white.

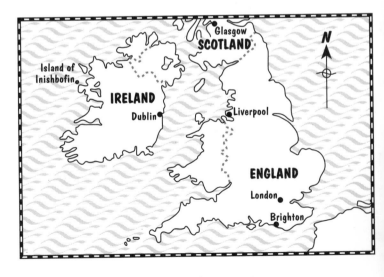

Chapter 1   *Light and darkness*

The man and the woman danced around the office holding each other. They smiled and laughed as they danced. They had their arms around each other. They danced and they danced. They did not want this moment to go away.

'We did it, John. We really did it.'

'I know we did, Jenny. I know.'

John was a television producer and Jenny was his assistant. They were getting excited about a series of six television programmes they had made. The series was called *Know your Mind, Love your Body.* It was about the relationship between the body and the mind. Each programme had looked at a different subject: other forms of medicine, meditation, yoga, a good diet and so on. It had not been an expensive series to make, but millions of people had watched it and the newspapers had talked a lot about it.

It had been John's idea. He felt there was a growing interest in the subject, but even he had been surprised by the size of the audiences and the interest in the newspapers.

'Tell me again what the boss said, John.'

'He said he thinks it's the best series he's seen since . . . ever. And he talked about how much the newspapers loved the programmes. Our managing director is a very, very happy man. He wants to talk to me about money, about my salary, about giving me a rise, would you believe?'

The smile disappeared from Jenny's face for a second when he talked about his salary.

'And a rise for you too, of course!' John added. Jenny's smile returned. 'He thinks it might win the Montreux Gold Prize for best documentary programme.'

'It's fantastic,' said Jenny. 'We did it. It's a success. We really did it.' Jenny was dancing by herself now.

'Of course it's successful,' John joked. 'We believed it would be successful, and it is successful. If you believe in something, it will happen. It may not happen exactly the way you want, but it will happen. If we believe that something is true, it becomes true. That's what the programmes were all about.'

'Have you talked to Rachel yet?' Jenny asked, bringing him back to the present.

'I haven't had a chance to phone Rachel yet. I've just got off the phone with the managing director, I haven't had a chance. I'll do it now. But listen, let's talk over lunch, I have an idea for another programme.'

Rachel was John's wife. She was the first person he always ran to talk to when he had good news, or bad news, or no news, or when he felt low, or when he felt good. They had been married for just under two years and in that time they had kept no secrets from each other. They had told each other everything. It was why their relationship was so good, so strong. They discussed how they felt, what they were thinking, what they had done. Everything. They had no secrets from each other.

He picked up the phone and turned his back on Jenny before she had even moved towards the door, but she didn't mind. Jenny knew him, she knew his love for his wife and son, she knew how excited he was. She left the room smiling to herself. All days should be like this, she thought. But no, then they wouldn't be special, and this was a special day.

John sat down at his desk with the phone in his hand. He looked happily around his office and out of the window. The views from his fourth-floor office were some of the best in London: The Houses of Parliament were to the west, Tower Bridge was so close you could imagine reaching out and touching it and the whole building overlooked the River Thames. The river was busy today; there were boats carrying tourists, and office workers having a birthday party on a hired pleasure boat. Even the river police looked relaxed today as they went up and down the river doing work that was often unpleasant.

John almost never took time to look out of the window. He sometimes asked himself why the television company had spent so much money on a building in this beautiful but expensive part of London. Everyone who worked in the building was either out making films or so busy in meetings that they never looked out to enjoy the view.

Probably the building with its views was for the visitors from other British and foreign television companies who came to buy their programmes. It was big, big money, and the least you could do for these important men and women was offer them such a view. Maybe it helped sell the programmes, especially on a beautiful spring morning like this.

At this moment, John felt very good about himself as he looked at his office, as he thought about the success of his programmes. But then he remembered the phone in his hand and that he wanted to talk to Rachel. He paused and put the phone down again.

John was worried about Rachel. She had not seemed happy for the last couple of weeks. She had seemed nervous, worried about something. Worried most of all about Patrick, their young son. She had not wanted to go out anywhere recently. He had gone out alone at least three times in the last two weeks. To a party, to a play, to dinner with friends. The kind of thing that Rachel loved. But she had not wanted to go out of the house. She had not wanted to leave Patrick.

Twice she had woken up screaming in the middle of the night after bad dreams and had jumped out of bed and run to Patrick's room. She had picked him up and held him tight in her arms. She had pushed her face against him, crying and shaking as she held him until slowly her crying stopped and she put him down gently in his bed. She had not returned to their bedroom and John had got up and gone to her and led her back to bed.

'What was it?' he asked as he put his arms around her and held her. 'What was it, my love, what happened?' he repeated.

'I don't know, I don't know. I just knew that something bad had happened to Patrick. I don't know what. I was looking for him, I couldn't find him anywhere. I don't know, I don't know, I don't know what it was. I was just so frightened.'

He held her again as she started to cry once more and held her like that until she fell asleep. At first she moved and even shook in his arms and then she fell into a more gentle sleep, her breath soft on his cheek.

When she had woken she had not wanted to talk about the dream, had not wanted to remember and so they had let it go. But later that same day she had run from their car with Patrick in her arms as John had started the engine. Since then she had refused to go anywhere in the car. Since then, if she had to go anywhere, she went on foot, carrying Patrick in her arms. She stopped every time a car came past, her lips pressed together in a tight line, her hands held around Patrick as if to protect him, as if she was afraid something was going to happen to him.

It was strange, John thought, to feel so successful and so worried at the same time. He picked up the phone again to call Rachel, his earlier excitement now gone, and he wondered what it was his wife was trying to protect Patrick from.

Chapter 2   *Happy birthday*

'You haven't forgotten the birthday this week,' said Rachel the moment she recognised his voice on the phone.

John didn't reply immediately. It was not that he had forgotten Patrick's birthday, more that he was surprised and pleased by the sound of her voice. She sounded happy, she sounded excited. She didn't sound worried. It was her old voice, her beautiful soft voice, and it felt to him like a ghost from the past, a very welcome ghost. His shoulders relaxed, he breathed out deeply and he smiled at the phone. He almost wanted to say 'welcome back', but he didn't want to talk about the last few weeks. He was afraid this moment might change, that by talking about it the worries and fears of the last few weeks might come back. Instead he said: 'Our son's first birthday, how could I forget that? What kind of father do you think I am?' His voice was light, cheerful as he continued. 'I just wasn't sure what to do for his birthday. I mean, this is a special day, for him, for all of us, and I just wanted to do something special and . . .'

The idea came to him as he spoke to her. Of course, it would be perfect.

'And I have an idea. Let's go to Ireland for a little holiday. Let's go back to our place, to the little island. I can't think of a better place to spend Patrick's birthday.'

'Wow! Are you serious? Can we? Can you really get time off work? When do we go?'

He laughed at her questions. One moment she didn't believe him, the next moment she was organising it all.

'Yes. Yes. Yes, my boss loves me. At the end of the week.' John answered the questions in turn and then added, 'I'll book tickets now and I'll tell you why my boss loves me later, when I get home.'

Ireland, the cliffs and the tiny island off the west coast. They had gone there for their first ever holiday together. A holiday where they had danced together at the top of the Cliffs of Moher, cliffs that stood straight out of the sea to a height of over one hundred metres. They had danced to the music he sang in her ear. Rachel was wearing a light white summer dress and he changed the words of a popular song and sang instead to his 'lady in white'.

'Ireland will be cold,' he had warned her. But he was happy to be wrong and he had held her close and felt her warm and soft against him. On that holiday they had decided to get married, and Patrick had been born less than nine months after the holiday. And so they called him Patrick, an Irish name. Yes, Ireland was a very special place for them.

'And you really can get time off work?'

'Yes, yes, yes. I told you, my boss loves me. I'm just going to have lunch with Jenny now and then I'll come home and we can plan our trip.'

'Let's hire a car when we get there and then we can drive around a bit.'

A car. It was her suggestion. She had seemed afraid of cars for the last few weeks and now she had suggested hiring one. She really was herself again, thought John, and he felt very pleased.

                    *   *   *

For lunch Jenny suggested a small Italian restaurant behind
St Paul's Cathedral. They took a taxi there. They were still
feeling very happy and excited about the success of their
series, and they laughed and joked like teenagers all the way
to the restaurant.

When they arrived they ordered a bottle of the
restaurant's best red wine. When the food came they ate
slowly, taking pleasure in the food. They did not often go
out for lunch. They normally had a sandwich at work, if
they ate anything at all. And when they did find time to go
out for lunch they usually ate quickly and talked and talked
without looking at what they were eating.

But this time the talk about work could wait until after
they had finished their meal and were relaxing over coffee.

'So, what's your new idea and why can't it wait until
tomorrow?' Jenny asked as she finished her rich cheesecake
and looked at the plate to make sure she had not missed
anything.

'It's not such a new idea. But anyway, first I have to tell
you that I'm taking a week off for a little holiday. So you
can work while I rest!'

She smiled at him and said, 'You rest and I work, there's
certainly nothing new about that. What's the idea?'

'Do you remember some time ago we talked about those
urban myths? You know, those stories that people tell in
different places all over the country. It's always the same
basic story, but the story is told as if it happened in that
place, in that town or village. You know what I mean? And
no-one is sure if they are actually true or not? Do you
remember?'

'Yeah, you mean like the story about the car in the middle of the forest,' she said.

'Which story is that?' John asked.

'You know, the story about the couple driving home late at night through a forest. They run out of petrol and the man goes to get some and the woman stays in the car. And she waits and waits and the man doesn't come back.' Jenny began to speak more quietly and more slowly as she got excited by her own storytelling. 'After a little while she hears a noise on the roof of the car. Like someone is knocking on the roof. And she's frightened and locks the doors and then a police car comes up behind. A policeman gets out of his car and shouts at her, "Get out of your car and walk towards me and don't look back" and . . .'

'Yeah, that sort of thing,' John said with a smile, but didn't let her finish. Jenny made a face as if she was disappointed not to be able to finish the story.

'That same story, and others like it are told in different towns all over Britain, as if they were true, but no-one can ever find any evidence for them, no police records, no hospital records, nothing. Well, my idea is to try to collect some more of these stories and find out where they come from. I want to see if people have always told stories like this and if they have, what stories they used to tell years ago. Maybe we could make a programme out of it. I don't know. What do you think?'

Jenny was nodding thoughtfully. 'Maybe,' she said. 'It just reminded me of something I read the other day about a mysterious hitch-hiker. You know the kind of thing?'

John shook his head gently as if he was thinking of something else, as if he was already on holiday.

'Well, you know what a hitch-hiker is, don't you?' Jenny asked, jokingly.

'I should know,' said John. 'That's how I met Rachel! That's how we met.' He smiled at the memory and Jenny realised the serious talk was over and that he wanted to get home to his wife and son.

'OK, I'll see what I can find. I'll do some work while you rest.'

'That's how we met,' was the thought in John's head as he left the restaurant. Hitch-hiking. That's how Rachel and he had met.

Chapter 3   *The lady in white*

It was Friday morning, John's last day at work before their holiday in Ireland. John had bought plane tickets to Ireland and booked the same cottage they had stayed in before, on a small island off the west coast of Ireland. He had also booked a car at Dublin Airport. Everything was ready and he was looking forward to the holiday. He was thinking about nothing else. He wasn't thinking about work when the telephone rang.

It was Jenny.

'You're still here, then?' she asked.

'Oh yes, I'll be here for some time yet.'

'I don't suppose you want to talk about work, do you?' she asked.

'Well, to be honest, not really,' he said 'Why? Do you have something you want to tell me?'

'Maybe.'

'Maybe?'

'Just something I thought you might be interested in,' Jenny said. 'Something I found about the urban myths we talked about the other day at lunch.'

'Really? You have been busy!'

'Well, I haven't been busy planning a holiday,' she laughed.

'OK. Thank you for that little joke. Now, what have you found?' John asked.

'Well, I telephoned different local newspapers and radio stations,' Jenny explained. 'I guessed that the local ones were more likely to cover these kinds of stories. I gave them the example stories we talked about and asked them to phone me if they had anything. I also looked through the Internet and checked the central library to see what books I could find.'

'And did you find anything?'

'A couple of interesting reports that I still want to check out and . . .' She paused. There was a long silence on the phone. She had obviously found something interesting and she was playing with him, making him wait. It was one of their games.

John laughed down the phone. He liked playing the game too so he waited a while before asking.

'And did you find anything interesting?'

'Yes.'

'So tell me,' John said.

'Do you have time?'

'Jenny!' he said in a louder voice that suggested he was becoming a little tired of the game.

'OK, OK. But not on the phone.'

'Why not on the phone?' he asked.

'Because I have something I want you to listen to as well.'

'OK, but come now. I really do have other things to do today. OK?'

The door of his office opened less than two minutes later and Jenny walked in.

John laughed again.

'You really don't waste time, do you?'

Jenny laughed back and put a cassette player on the desk in front of him.

'What's this?' John asked.

'I'll play it to you in a minute, but let me just tell you how I found it first, OK?' she said.

'OK.'

'Here it is. It's the hitch-hiker story I mentioned on Tuesday. I found three hitch-hiker stories from different local newspapers or radio stations in different parts of the country. I mean, really different parts of the country. One from Glasgow, one from Liverpool and one from a small village outside Cambridge. But . . .' and she paused again, keeping John waiting again, '. . . the stories are exactly the same . . . *exactly* the same. Three different men in three different places all telling exactly the same story.'

'Maybe they know each other,' he said.

'I don't think so. Like I say, they live in different parts of the country. They work in quite different jobs and the stories they tell happened in different years. But, anyway, the really interesting thing is, they all say this happened to them in exactly the same place, just north of Brighton.'

'So, why did they come to Brighton?' he asked. 'I mean it's one of my favourite places for a weekend out of London, but what about them?'

'Again, different reasons. One man was on business. Another had taken his daughter back to the university there and the third . . .' she checked her notes, '. . . had been to a football match.'

'So, what *did* happen to them?'

'Well, listen for yourself,' Jenny said as she took a cassette from her jacket pocket and put it in the cassette player.

'This is from the local radio station in Liverpool. They talked to one of the men. I don't think they took it very seriously. They used it as part of a programme at Halloween. You know, all about ghost stories and things like that. But, of course, the radio station didn't know about the other two men. Anyway, they sent me this yesterday. I think you'll find it interesting.'

'Let's listen,' said John pressing the play button himself. He wanted to hear the story, but he also wanted to get away from work and start his holiday as soon as possible.

The cassette was silent for a moment and then the recording began. The interviewer spoke first.

So tell us what actually happened.

Well, I was driving back from Brighton. I had taken my daughter there, back to the university. She's twenty-two but my wife still worries a lot about her so I drive her there myself. And I was on my way back home. It's a long drive but I like driving at night. Less traffic. The weather was good. It was a clear, dry night. And I had just driven through a small village and was still going quite slowly and then, just outside the village I saw a woman. She was standing at the side of the road and . . . all dressed in white she was, so I saw her immediately. And as I drove past she put her hand out as if she was hitch-hiking and I stopped. I mean, I don't normally stop for hitch-hikers because, well you never know who you're going to pick up, do you? But, a woman, late at night, and I thought of my daughter and I know how I would feel if she was out by herself late at night, so I stopped.

And then?

She walked up behind the car. I opened the door and asked her where she was going. 'The nearest garage, please,' she said. So I said, 'Get in.' She said, 'Thank you.' She got in and I drove on. I saw that she hadn't put on her seat belt. I mentioned this to her and she looked at me and then started crying. She didn't say anything at all, she just started crying. She didn't say a word, she just started crying. I didn't know what was going on. I asked her, 'Are you all right?' but she obviously wasn't and she didn't answer and she just kept on crying. I didn't know what to do. I didn't know what to say. I just drove on, I didn't know if I should stop or . . . or, do something else. I just didn't know. And I had just about decided to stop the car when she said, 'I'm sorry I . . .' and she was still breathing really fast, as if she was fighting to breathe. But she had stopped crying. I still felt like my stomach was in my mouth and my hair was standing on end . . . I didn't know what to do.

And then she said, 'I'm sorry, I'm sorry. We had a bit of a problem with the car. That's why I'm going to the garage. The others are waiting at the car. I don't know why I started crying like that. I'm sorry.' I asked if I could help with the car. I asked her where the car was and she said, 'No, thank you. The garage will be able to help.' And she said the car was just outside the village where I had stopped for her. Well, I didn't remember seeing any other car parked on the road outside the village, but I didn't want to disagree with her, you know. I didn't want her to start crying again. She was quiet again and then I noticed she was shaking. 'Are you cold? I can put the heater on.' She thanked me and said it was because of the rain and how she was still wet. I turned to look at her for a moment and noticed her face was wet, and her hair, and her dress. 'Was it raining here?' I asked. Because I had not seen a drop of rain that day, anywhere.

John put his hand on the cassette player and pressed a button. The tape stopped.

'He hasn't finished yet,' Jenny said.

'Where did you get this?' John's voice was strange, very cold.

Jenny looked at him. He had a strange look on his face. Jenny had never seen John like this, had never heard his voice like this. She felt suddenly cold all down her back. His voice and his look made her feel uncomfortable. They made her feel more frightened than the story on the cassette had.

'I told you, from Liverpool. From the local radio station there.'

John was staring at the cassette player. He was very still and his face had gone completely white.

'What's the matter, John? Are you OK? John?'

He didn't seem to hear her and continued to sit still for a few moments and then he looked up at her.

'What's going on here? Is this some kind of a joke? Is this your joke?'

'No. What do you mean, joke? What are you talking about? John, what are you talking about? There's no joke. John, you're frightening me. What do you mean?'

He looked at her for a minute, not speaking, just staring at her, as if he was trying to see inside her, to see what she was thinking. Then he nodded his head slowly as if to show he believed that she was not playing a joke on him.

'Maybe he knows me.'

'Who? Maybe who knows you?'

He looked towards the cassette player. 'Him. The man telling this story. But, why would he do this?'

'Do what? What are you talking about John?' she asked, worried. This was not a joke, not her joke and clearly it was not a joke for him either.

'This is *my* story,' he said so softly she hardly heard him, and then he repeated it a little louder. 'This is *my story.*'

'Your story? But how? I told you, John. There were three men. They all told the same story. How could it be your story?'

Again John was silent, sitting and staring at the desk. It was impossible to know what was going on in his head. He was shaking his head from side to side now as if he was trying hard to understand something.

'What's going on here? I don't understand this. This is my story. How did he know this? How? I don't understand.'

They sat for some time on opposite sides of the desk without speaking. Jenny sat looking at John. She was worried. She was also a little frightened. She didn't know what to do. Should she get help? Leave him? Stay with him? Say something? Get him a drink? What should she do? What could she do . . . ?

Chapter 4 *Losing control*

Jenny was still trying to decide what to do when John suddenly moved his hand out towards the cassette player and pressed the play button again. The voice on the cassette continued telling the story.

. . . *And she said it had been raining all day and maybe that was why they had the problem with the car. And then she went quiet and I was afraid she might start crying again so I didn't say anything more. I didn't ask any more questions. I just drove. And it was a lovely night, I couldn't understand how it could have been raining here because the road was as dry as . . . I don't know what, but it was just very dry.*

And then, after a while, I felt that she was looking at me again. I tried not to notice. I didn't want to look back at her. I mean she was really beautiful. I noticed that the minute she got into the car. Really beautiful. Dark hair and clear blue eyes. I could see them when I opened the door and the light came on inside the car. Really lovely. And normally I would have been very happy to look at her, and for her to look at me. But there was something very strange about this whole situation and it was beginning to make me feel nervous.

And I was beginning to wonder why she was crying about a car. I mean I know it's a problem when something goes wrong with your car, especially at night, but it is only a machine, isn't it? And you can get it repaired and . . . and there must be a garage somewhere around here. So I was thinking 'Why is she crying about this?' And then I thought, 'Maybe it's not the car, maybe something else has happened, maybe she was with a man or something and he . . . and he did something. . .' And so I was about to ask her . . . if she really was all right and I turned to look at her and she was looking at me.

She was looking at me . . . it's difficult to describe the look but . . . I don't know what it was, it was like she was trying to see what kind of person I was. It was, I don't know, it was almost sexy and yet uncertain, as if she didn't know if she could trust me or not. I mean, after the tears and everything, it made me feel sort of excited and nervous at the same time. And a bit uncomfortable. I mean, she was not much older than my daughter.

Anyway, I didn't like her looking at me like that, and I looked away, back to the road. When I saw the sign that said there was a garage in five hundred metres, I felt almost happy. I just wanted to get her out of the car. I said, 'We'll soon be there,' but she didn't answer. Then suddenly, as I was getting close to a bend in the road, she started to scream. I went cold inside and my stomach jumped and she was screaming, 'Oh God, we're losing control, we're losing control, watch out, watch out, oh my God!'

And I was just staring at the road, and . . . nothing. There was nothing there. The road was empty, the car was going the same as before. There was nothing. Nothing was happening. So I turned to look at her, and as I did, she suddenly put her hands on the steering wheel of the car and pulled it . . .

John had been sitting listening quietly to the story without moving, but now he suddenly changed his position

23

in his chair. He shook his head a few times, as if he was disagreeing with someone.

'No, it wasn't like that. No, it wasn't like that. No, she didn't do that, no.'

Jenny sat staring at him. What was John talking about? What did he mean? She watched as he moved closer to the cassette player, as if to listen more carefully, although the man continued to speak in the same way, not louder, not quieter. And then the man's voice suddenly did rise and he almost shouted as he relived the memory.

. . . I shouted at her, 'Stop it, stop it! What are you doing? Do you want to kill us?' The car was moving from side to side as she pulled on the steering wheel and I tried to keep the car straight on the road. She was strong. She was really strong. I couldn't believe it. She wasn't big and she was quite slim. I don't know where she got the strength from. It was really difficult. I pulled the steering wheel as hard as I could with my right hand and hit her arm with my left hand.

There was a pause in the recording as if the man was embarrassed at the memory of hitting a woman, a young woman. A young woman like his own daughter, perhaps. The interviewer then asked:

And then?

The car was still going from side to side. I put my foot on the brake, really hard. But with her still pulling on the wheel and me standing on the brakes like that, the car just turned round. I lost control. I really did lose control. I tried to control

24

the car again but I couldn't. The car hit the grass at the side of the road, and jumped in the air and hit the grass again and then came to a stop. I just sat there, staring at the road, not moving. My hands were still on the steering wheel, holding it really tightly. And then, then I just blew out all the air that was inside me. It was as if I had been holding my breath all this time and my heart was going like a train. I could hear it, I could hear my heart beating as if the noise was coming from outside my body. And my hands were completely wet on the steering wheel, and I just sat there and then . . . and then I remembered her.

'What was that all about?' I shouted at her. 'Why did you do that? What's the matter with you?' But she just sat there, looking straight in front of her with her hand over her mouth. And then she pushed the hair from her face and I saw something on her face. Something dark was running down her face from her hair. I think it was blood. So I felt bad about shouting at her. I asked her how she was, but I think my voice was still loud. She looked at me. She looked so frightened. And then she looked away from me and she tried to open the door. At first she couldn't find the handle, but then she did find it and she managed to open the door.

She was out of the car and running back down the road before I had a chance to say anything more. I shouted something. I don't know what. I don't know what I shouted and then I tried to open my door but my seat belt was stuck – I couldn't take it off at first – and then I did get it off. I opened the door and jumped out of the car and I ran after her. I got round the bend in the road and kept running and . . . and then . . . then I just stopped. She had gone. Disappeared. There was nothing. Nobody. Just a straight, empty road. And

I mean, she was wearing white, you know. It was a perfectly clear night. But I couldn't see her. She wasn't there. And there were no other roads, no turnings. There was nothing at the side of the road, just an open field, on both sides of the road. It just wasn't possible for her to disappear. I just stood there, looking all around me and then a car came racing towards me along the road. Its lights almost blinded me and the driver blew his horn as he drove past. He probably thought I was drunk. I felt as if I was drunk. I felt very strange.

I walked back to the car and sat there for a while, staring at nothing. But then two more cars came round the corner and blew their horns at me. Then I realised my car was facing the wrong direction and I kind of woke up. I decided to drive back and see what I could find. I drove as far as the village where I had picked her up, but there was nothing. No lady in white, no cars parked at the side of the road with people waiting in them. Nothing. I didn't know what to do. Report it to the police? Report what? That I gave a young woman a lift in the car, that she cried, that she went mad and almost caused an accident? That she disappeared into thin air? I couldn't! I couldn't. . .

But I couldn't drive on either, and it was too late to find a hotel or anything like that. I decided to stop and try to get some sleep in the car and then drive on. But I didn't want to stop near that village. I don't know why, but I was afraid. I didn't know what to think, but I was sure I didn't want to see that woman again.

It was Jenny who turned the cassette player off. She had heard it before and knew the man had finished his story.

There was silence in the room. As the man had told his

story Jenny had not taken her eyes off John. As the man had talked about the accident John had continued to shake his head, and whispered 'No, no' a couple more times. Now he just sat there, not moving, not saying anything, just staring at the cassette player. Jenny was feeling very uncomfortable. While the man had been telling his story on the cassette she had not felt so bad, but now that the voice on the cassette had stopped, now that there was just John and her in the room, she felt very alone. She wanted to ask him to explain but she was afraid. She had never seen him like this. He sat there in his own world and she was afraid to ask him any more questions.

They continued to sit there for some time and then John took a deep, deep breath, then another, and then he looked up at her. His face was very calm now.

'Get your car keys,' he said quietly. 'I'll drive. And bring your mobile phone, we'll need it, and the telephone numbers of those three men. Have you got them?'

She nodded and was pleased that she had the telephone numbers, pleased that she did not have to speak. She did not know if she could control her voice.

'Come on,' he said and got up and walked quickly towards the door.

She didn't ask him where they were going. She was still not sure about her voice. She also had a feeling that she already knew where they were going, but she couldn't quite believe it.

Chapter 5 *A journey into the past*

They drove across Waterloo Bridge and down the busy main road to the large roundabout at Elephant and Castle, that strangely named part of London south of the river. There was no elephant and no castle, just a lot of dirty, grey office buildings with a large shopping centre in the middle of a very large roundabout.

It was at the roundabout that Jenny saw a road sign for Brighton. 'So, we are going there,' she thought. 'We are going to the village where these men met the hitch-hiker.'

She looked at John, but he said nothing. He continued to look straight ahead.

They drove on. Jenny looked out the window. No tourists ever came to this part of the city. There was nothing of interest here, only large areas of houses and flats. Every few kilometres there was a little group of shops in streets that were always called High Street. The streets all looked the same. The shops too were always the same; Boots, W. H. Smith, Woolworths. You could be in any part of London or in any town in Britain and find exactly the same shops.

There was nothing of interest here for Jenny either but she looked at everything she passed as if she had never been here in her life. It was better to watch everything they passed than to think of what they were doing, to think of where they were going. It was better to do this than try to guess what was going on in John's mind.

She had worked with John for over three years. They knew each other very well. She had often thought she knew what John was thinking. She could sometimes finish his sentences for him. But now, she had no idea what he was thinking. She was not sure if she wanted to know what he was thinking.

He drove in complete silence, not even saying a word as the driver of another car pulled out suddenly in front of them and John had to brake quickly. This reminded Jenny to put on her seat belt and, as she put it on, she thought of the story on the cassette. The man had said something about a seat belt in the story. She tried to remember exactly what he had said, but the only thing that came to her mind was the question she had been asking herself since they left the office.

What did John mean when he said 'This is my story'? What was in this story that had made her boss turn white and go silent? She had never known John to remain silent for so long. He normally talked a lot and was quiet only when he was trying to understand something. He still looked at her at those times, even if he said nothing. But now his face showed nothing. He stared straight in front of the car. Jenny returned her attention to what was outside the car.

They were on the road that took them around Croydon, to the south of London. They drove past the old airport that had once been London's main airport. This was where the British prime minister, Neville Chamberlain, had returned to after a meeting with Hitler before the 1939–45 war. He had waved a piece of paper as he climbed down from the plane. A piece of paper that Hitler had signed. 'Peace in our time' is what Chamberlain had said of this agreement he had signed with Hitler. Jenny could see the picture in her head, although all of this had happened long before she was born. Even her father had only been a child when all this had happened. It was a story Jenny knew from other people, but it was not her story, it did not touch her in any direct way. It was not *her* story.

'This is *my* story,' John had said.

She could not get the sentence out of her head. She could still hear John's voice as he had said this and the disbelief on his face. She could not get this out of her head. What did he mean?

Journalists sometimes said 'This is my story' when they were writing about something and they did not want other journalists to write about it. But John had not meant that. He and Jenny worked together on stories, there was no competition between them. So what did he mean?

They were leaving the city behind them as they travelled south. They left the rows of small houses with living rooms that were only a few metres away from the speeding traffic, houses with no gardens for children to play in. It wasn't a safe place for children with all this traffic. Now the houses were big with big gardens. Then they were in the open countryside, with less traffic and more signs for Brighton. They were getting close.

Just before they joined the motorway, she noticed a car parked at the side of the road and a man standing looking at it. She watched him in the side mirror as they drove past without slowing down. He was standing looking at the engine. He was well dressed and she guessed he did not know much about engines. She smiled as she thought of herself in similar situations. She also knew nothing about cars. She remembered being with a boyfriend once in his car. They had gone for a walk in a forest park. A beautiful place, she remembered. But when they got back to the car and tried to start the engine, nothing happened. Her boyfriend had looked at the engine and, although he found the problem quickly, he had not been able to repair it himself.

'I have an idea,' he had said to her, 'you stay here and look at the engine helplessly, I'll go over to that café. I need the toilet anyway.'

Jenny had wondered what he was talking about. But within two minutes another man had appeared from nowhere and had offered to help her, and had repaired the car. She smiled again at the memory. She had not seen much of that boyfriend after that and she had always bought the best cars she could afford for herself. She didn't want to break down in the middle of the night somewhere, in the middle of nowhere. Not like that lady in white, hitch-hiking on a lonely road at night.

The smile disappeared from Jenny's face as she remembered something else now, something John had said in that Italian restaurant. Something about Rachel. Something he had said when they were talking about hitch-hiking. Yes, now she remembered his words. He had said, 'That's how Rachel and I met. Hitch-hiking. That's how we met.'

Jenny suddenly felt cold inside. 'That's my story.' John's words came back to her again and slowly a new question entered Jenny's mind. Was it possible that John had met

Rachel in the same way that the man on the cassette had described?

'That's not possible.'

She realised that she had said these words out loud and had not thought them silently. She turned nervously towards John, but he continued to stare ahead as if he had heard nothing. She was happy he had not heard. She did not want to tell him what she was thinking. She was not sure herself what she was thinking. The same phrase continued in her head, repeated again and again. 'That's not possible. That's not possible.'

What had she thought as she had listened to the voice on the cassette and heard the stories from the other two men? That this was an interesting example of how the same story can travel from place to place, all over the country, and be retold in exactly the same way, as if it was true, as if it really happened? Had she for a moment thought that there was some truth in the story itself? What truth? That this woman was a ghost?

'That's not possible.'

Again she was not sure if she had spoken out loud or just thought this, or if indeed John had spoken these words. She turned and looked at him. He was shaking his head slowly from side to side, as if he was also thinking, 'That's not possible.' Had John actually spoken these words? Was John thinking the same thoughts as her?

But she had no time to think any more about it. At the side of the road she saw the name of the next village. She recognised the name of the village from the men's story. They were arriving in the village where the three men had met the hitch-hiker.

She sat completely still as John drove into the village. He continued to drive without slowing down and a new thought came to her suddenly. The man on the cassette had not mentioned the name of the village! *She* knew it from what the reporters from the local radio stations had told her. The man on the cassette had not mentioned the name, and she had not told John.

'So maybe we are not going to stop here,' she thought. 'Maybe we are going somewhere else. Maybe this is not the same as John's story.' As these thoughts filled her head, John looked in the car's rear-view mirror, slowed down and turned the car round. He drove back through the village and stopped just outside it on the other side of the road from where Jenny had seen the name of the village.

And then John spoke to her, for the first time since they had left the office. His voice was quiet and calm.

'This is where I first met Rachel. This is where I first met my wife. She was hitch-hiking. She was standing right there. I was driving back to London. I stopped my car. She was standing right there. I gave her a lift. She was wearing a dress. She was wearing a white dress. She was standing right there . . .'

Chapter 6   *The policeman's story – the accident*

Jenny was speaking on her mobile telephone. She was standing a couple of metres away from John, who watched and listened as she spoke. It was his idea to phone one of the three men who had met the hitch-hiker. That is why he had told her to bring the phone and the telephone numbers as they left the office. She was talking to one of the men. She had tried another number already but there was no answer. With the second number the phone was answered almost immediately and the man was pleased to hear from her.

John could only hear Jenny's part of the conversation.

'Yes, we're just outside the village.'

'Yes, going north towards London.'

Jenny turned round to look at something behind her.

'Yes, I can see that.'

'Yes.'

'OK, thank you for your help.'

'Yes, I'll phone you if we decide to make the programme.'

'Thank you. Yes, goodbye. No, I don't think that will be necessary. Goodbye.'

Jenny put the phone back in her jacket pocket.

She and John stood looking at each other for a moment.

'So this is the place where he met the hitch-hiker?' John asked.

'Yeah. This is the place.'

'He's sure?' John asked.

'He said he would never forget this place. Yes, it's the same place,' Jenny replied.

'And the same place where I met Rachel.'

Jenny did not know what to say. What did this all mean? What did it mean that Rachel and John had met at the same place where the three men had met the mysterious hitch-hiker?

They continued to look at each other without speaking. Neither of them knew what to say and neither of them seemed to know what to do now. Finally Jenny broke the silence.

'I'm going to phone the police,' she said.

'Why?'

Jenny didn't answer John. She didn't know herself why she was phoning the police. She just knew she had to do something. She didn't want to stand there alone with John in the silence of his unspoken thoughts and her own unspoken thoughts. When she felt uncomfortable in a situation Jenny always had to do something. She hated uncomfortable silences. It always made her feel better to move, to do something. Usually what she did was to run away as fast as she could. She had left many boyfriends like that. But, although she felt uncomfortable here, this was her work – she could not leave John alone.

She phoned the operator and got the number of the police station in Brighton. The police in Brighton suggested she talked to the local police in a village a few kilometres away. They told her how to get there.

*   *   *

It took them a long time to find the police station, although the village was not large. The police station was an ordinary-looking house, a house in its own garden. A car stood outside. It was a blue car, very clean with nothing lying around inside, no cassettes, no magazines, no waste paper. It didn't look like a family car but it also didn't look like the normal white police cars with their bright red and blue markings. The word 'Police' was written in quite small letters on the side of the car and nowhere else. The Police sign on the wall just beside the front door was also small.

It was difficult to believe that it really was a police station at all. But when the door opened there was a policeman in his dark blue uniform standing there. He was a middle-aged man, probably in his late fifties. He smiled at them. Jenny imagined that not many people came to see him – it didn't look like a busy police station. The policeman invited them into a small office and then into the living room beside it.

'We'll be more comfortable in here,' he said.

Jenny was not surprised when the policeman offered a cup of tea before they could explain why they were there. Jenny accepted. She was doing all the talking and John sat down without saying anything. This was not the normal John, the John who liked to lead, who liked to take control. Jenny again remembered words from the story on the cassette. 'We're losing control. We're losing control.' She wondered for a moment if John was also losing control. She had never seen him like this. She had never seen him so quiet, not speaking, hardly moving.

While the policeman was out in the kitchen Jenny looked around his room. It was also very tidy. It was the room of a man who had lived alone for many years. There were only a few personal things and nothing looked out of place. There was a bookcase in the corner where all the books stood in perfect order. There were no books lying on their sides, no spaces between the books, they were all standing up straight. For a moment Jenny wondered if they were real books at all, but she didn't check.

She looked instead at the three photographs on the small table beside the television. They were all black-and-white photographs. Two showed young couples, different couples, both staring back at the photographer and smiling. In one photo the couple were formally dressed and it looked as if it had been taken by a professional photographer. From their clothes it looked as if it had been taken in the 1930s.

The photograph of the second couple was taken much later Jenny thought, and was more relaxed. On holiday somewhere, a couple with the sea behind them. The third photo showed a very young boy, perhaps only one year old. Jenny looked at the photographs and tried to imagine the relationships with the policeman. Were the older couple his parents? Were the other couple the policeman himself with his wife? Where was she now? Was the boy the policeman's son? There were no other photographs.

She wondered if his story was happy or not. She hoped it was happy. She looked at John as the policeman brought the tea. John, she thought, was looking at the picture of the young boy. The boy was probably about the same age as Patrick she thought. Yes, she hoped this would be a happy story.

*   *   *

37

The policeman looked thoughtful as Jenny explained why they had come and told him the story of the mysterious hitch-hiker.

'Have you heard any stories like that around?' Jenny asked him.

The policeman smiled.

'Well, I can't say that I have. It's very quiet round here, not a lot happens, so if something does happen, everyone talks about it, you know what I mean,' and he laughed quietly. 'This is a quiet place. If anything happens people love to talk about it, to gossip. So I'm sure I would have heard any ghost stories.'

Jenny thought he looked quickly at the photograph of the young couple near the sea, but she was more interested in what he had said. 'Ghost.' The word that neither she nor John had spoken. The word that she had not wanted to think and certainly not to say, not since John had listened to the story on the cassette. Not since John had said, 'This is my story.'

The policeman continued talking as John looked towards Jenny.

'You say they met this woman near the village? All three of the men met her in the same place?'

'Four.'

The policeman looked at John and John repeated, 'Four. Four men met her.'

'I'm sorry, I thought you said three men had reported this incident,' said the policeman as he looked again at Jenny. For the first time he sounded almost formal, more like a normal policeman.

'Maybe four,' said Jenny and then quickly continued.

38

'But, yes, in the same place, just north of the village, near the sign for the village actually.'

'Near that sign, you say?' He thought for a while, his face showing the effort he was making as he tried to remember. Then his wide smile appeared again – he had remembered.

'Yes, there was something, of course there was, I'd forgotten.'

He had been looking up at the ceiling as he tried to remember. Now, as his eyes came down and he looked at Jenny, the smile disappeared completely.

'It was an accident,' he said and he looked down at the floor. 'A terrible accident.' He looked as if he would rather not say anything more about it, as if remembering the accident had brought back feelings that were very painful.

He got up and went out to his office and when he returned after a few minutes he was carrying some papers. He sat down and started to speak, not touching the papers that lay on his knees.

'It was what we call an SCA.' And again his voice was more formal. 'That's what we call it, an SCA. A Single Car Accident. Just one car. They happen. Sometimes the driver is drunk. Sometimes it might even be someone trying to kill themselves. Suicide.'

He looked up at Jenny as he said this and then added quickly, 'I'm sorry, Miss, I didn't mean to suggest that happened in this case. I'm sure this had nothing to do with drink or . . . or with suicide. It's just that sometimes . . .'

He didn't finish the sentence. He seemed worried about Jenny. It was as if he was talking to the family of someone who had been in a road accident and not to television journalists. Jenny nodded her head and smiled at the policeman. She normally didn't like people calling her 'Miss'. She certainly did not like people behaving differently towards her because she was a woman. But she couldn't get angry with this friendly policeman who looked so unhappy himself at the memory of this accident.

'Go on,' she whispered.

'The driver seemed to lose control coming around the bend out of the village. Maybe she was going too fast, maybe something happened inside the car. We don't know. We checked the car afterwards and couldn't find anything wrong with the brakes or the steering wheel. It's difficult to tell though, after that kind of accident.'

He looked at them.

'Do you really want to know more about this?' he asked.

Jenny nodded. The policeman continued.

'It had been a very rainy night.'

John sat forward in his chair as the policeman said this. It was the first time he had moved since he had sat down in the policeman's living room, the first time he had shown that he was listening, that he was interested.

'Very wet,' the policeman continued, 'and the car left the road and hit a tree and that was it. They . . . they were both killed immediately.'

'They?' John and Jenny asked together.

'The woman . . . and . . . and the child. People from the village heard the crash and ran out. There was a doctor who lived nearby but . . . but there was nothing he could do. Nothing. They were both dead.'

'How old was the boy?' asked John looking at the photograph on the policeman's table.

The policeman looked surprised by the question.

'I didn't say it was a boy. How did you know that?'

John didn't say anything, but Jenny felt her heart sink as the policeman answered John's question.

'Just a baby. He wasn't even one year old.'

'Just like my son Patrick,' said John, 'just like Patrick.'

Chapter 7   *John's story*

The policeman continued to speak. He did not look at the papers on his knees but stared into space as if this helped him remember. He spoke calmly and without pausing.

'We tried to get in touch with her family, but we couldn't find anyone. There was an address in London on her driving licence. The police in London went to the house. They talked to neighbours. They said she had only lived there for a few months. Lived alone. I mean, she and the baby lived alone. They said she was very quiet, that she didn't go out much.

'She was always friendly when she met the neighbours outside, but she didn't talk much about herself. She obviously loved the baby. She seemed happy. The neighbours hadn't noticed any visitors coming to the house. They were surprised that there was no man around. You know how people are. They see a woman with a young baby and they wonder why there's no man around. But anyway, they hadn't seen any man or any other visitors, except the week before the accident.

'The neighbours said a young woman had come to stay about a week earlier. They looked very like each other, the two women. The neighbours thought that maybe they were sisters. The other woman looked as if she had come from a hot country, they said. She was very brown, very sun-tanned. And the police found a half-packed suitcase in the flat. They didn't know whose case it was. There was no address on it, nothing. They couldn't even tell if it was half packed or half unpacked, if someone had just arrived or if someone was planning to leave.

They checked the Registry Office in London, and found dates of birth for the woman and a sister. They also found records of their parents' deaths. But that was all they found. The Tax Office had records for the woman but not the sister. The records showed she had worked for a computer company for two years, but then left. The company didn't know any more about her. And that was it. That's all we ever found out. A single car accident. A woman and baby killed. No family found. Sad. Very sad.'

There was a long silence now. The policeman looked at the floor as he finished his story. Then he turned and looked again towards the photographs. As he moved in his chair, the papers fell from his knees and the noise seemed to wake him from his thoughts. He bent down to pick them up. He stopped as something on one of the pages caught his eye. He nodded his head and spoke softly, almost to himself.

'Of course, the other woman.'

He looked up at them, still nodding his head as he remembered.

'There was something else. Something a bit strange. Some of the villagers remembered seeing a young woman by the car. She was a stranger. I mean they didn't know her, she wasn't from the village. She was standing a few metres away from the car. She wasn't looking at the car, she was just standing, holding her handbag close to her chest and she was crying. One of the villagers put an arm round her, trying to make her feel better. He didn't know if she had been in the car or not. Or maybe from another car that had seen the accident and had stopped.'

The policeman paused, trying to remember more and then when he couldn't, he looked through the papers for a minute. He seemed disappointed that his memory had failed him. Then he continued.

'The ambulance arrived soon after and the villager went to help. He told the ambulance people about the other woman. He thought that maybe they should look at her and make sure that she was all right. But they couldn't find her. They looked for her but they couldn't find her.'

He looked again at the papers and read aloud: 'A young woman, dressed in white, was also seen near the scene of the accident but she left before any police officer was able to talk to her.'

*   *   *

Jenny drove away from the police station with John sitting in the passenger seat. They drove back to the village where the accident had happened. They drove past the place where they had stopped earlier. The place where John had given Rachel a lift. Neither of them spoke. They drove on and, after a few minutes, came to a petrol station.

'Stop here,' John said.

Jenny parked the car behind the petrol station. Even before the car had stopped John had started speaking, and speaking very quickly.

'This is where I dropped Rachel that night. I dropped her here and this is different from the other men's stories. This is different. I gave her a lift and she was wet and she was wearing a white dress. We had the same conversation about the car, the same as the man on the cassette said. She did start crying. All that was the same. She did look at me the way that man on the cassette described. But I looked back at her and we smiled. We smiled at each other and then we came here and I stopped.'

So, this is what John had meant by 'This is my story', Jenny thought. In a way she was not surprised by what he had just told her.

'She didn't shout anything? She didn't put her hands on the steering wheel?'

'No, no. Nothing like that. I left her here. I asked her again if she was sure I couldn't help. She said "no", she said "thank you", she smiled, she got out of the car. But she didn't close the door immediately. She seemed to be waiting for something. And I just asked her if, maybe, I could see her again. I said I would like to phone her some time to make sure . . .'

John smiled at the memory. This was the first smile Jenny had seen from him for a long time and she reached out her hand and touched him on the arm.

'I wanted to see her again,' John said.

'And you did, you did see her again and . . .' Jenny stopped. She had no idea how to continue.

John put his hands up to his face. Jenny was not sure if he was crying or not, but when he spoke again his voice was breaking.

'What the hell is this all about, Jenny? What does all this have to do with me, with Rachel? What does this all mean? I don't understand what's going on here. This is crazy. I don't believe this. I don't . . . I don't know what to believe.'

'What do you want it to mean, for God's sake?' Jenny

was almost shouting at him now. She was not angry with him, but shouting at him like this gave her more confidence in what she was saying.

'You met Rachel on the road, she said she had a problem with her car. You gave her a lift to the petrol station. You thought she was beautiful. She *is* beautiful. You wanted to see her again. You asked her out. You did see her again. You fell in love. You . . . you know what happened after that. What else do you want to think? Why do you want to think anything else?'

'And these other men's stories?' he asked.

'Their story is similar to yours, yes, but there are differences. You said that yourself. There are differences. I know it's unusual. It's strange, but that's all it is. Something very unusual, but it doesn't mean anything. Their stories have nothing to do with you.'

'And what about their stories?' John asked. 'What do you think happened to them? Who do you think their lady in white was? What does your journalist's mind have to say about that?'

Jenny paused, but only for a moment. She liked being a journalist.

'The woman. You know, the woman at the accident. That could have been the sister. The sister of the woman in the car. Maybe she was in the car too. Maybe she lost her memory because of the accident. It happens to people in accidents. They don't know where they are or who they are. Sometimes they lose their memory for a long time. So this woman is in shock. She walks off into the night. I don't know where to, and she doesn't know where she is going either. She just walks off, somewhere. Maybe someone gave her a lift. Maybe someone found her and helped her, but she couldn't remember anything. Later, she remembers this place. She doesn't remember anything else but she does remember this place, so she comes back here. She hopes she will remember everything. It happens. People in accidents hit their heads, they lose their memories. No-one is looking for her. Her only relative is killed in the accident, so no-one reports her missing. It happens.'

Jenny's voice was getting excited now, caught up by her own storytelling again.

'Anyway, she comes back, she comes back to this place. She remembers it, she remembers getting a lift from somewhere near here. She wants to remember the rest. That's why she comes back here. She doesn't know who she is or what she has lost, she doesn't know what has happened to her. She doesn't know anything. It's not just her memory she's looking for, there could be people out there waiting for her, looking for her, she doesn't know. She hopes that maybe coming back here and getting another lift will help her remember. So she tries. She tries again and again and again.'

'Until she meets me?'

'Will you get this out of your head? We are not talking about Rachel!' Jenny was almost screaming at John now. 'This is a *different* person. The fact that you met Rachel here is just a coincidence! Cars do break down, you know, and women do get wet in the rain, and you know perfectly well that it can be raining here and completely dry down the road. This is England, not the Sahara Desert!'

She was angry with him now, but she wasn't sure why. Maybe it was because she was frightened, frightened that

John wouldn't believe her, frightened because she didn't know if she believed it herself.

'And the lady in white always disappears?'

'She does *not* disappear, John! She runs away from an accident she has almost caused. She is frightened, she doesn't remember her past. All she remembers is that she is coming here again and again and the same thing is happening, as if it was out of her control. And she is frightened and she runs away. And hides in a field or somewhere, anywhere. She does not want to explain to the driver what this is all about.'

Jenny sat back in the seat of the car, exhausted by her own storytelling. And yet, she thought, her story could be true. She wanted to believe that. The thought that her story was true was calming her. And it was calming John. He sat beside her, nodding his head.

'What else do you want to believe?' Jenny continued, facing her own unbelievable and unspoken fears. 'That Rachel is a ghost? Go home, put your arms round her . . . and Patrick. If Rachel is a ghost what does that make Patrick? That's madness, John, that's madness. Go home, hold her in your arms and then phone me and tell me she's a ghost. OK?'

She laughed, although it was not a very natural laugh. She looked at John and she thought, she hoped, that she saw the beginning of a small smile appear in John's eyes.

'Go home to your family. Go on your holiday to Ireland. Get away from work. Get away from this story. You've been working too hard, for too long without a holiday. Go away and don't come back until you've forgotten all this.'

Chapter 8 *Ireland - peace and memories*

The boat left the small Irish fishing port and turned into the open Atlantic Ocean towards the island of Inishbofin. The weather was beautiful, a warm sunny day with almost no wind. The sea rose gently and slowly as if it were taking long slow breaths. Rachel stood at the back of the boat with Patrick in her arms. Patrick stared at the birds that followed the boat, sometimes flying so close to the boat that Patrick could almost touch them, smiling, happy, excited by his birthday present. John hoped the holiday would be a wonderful present for all of them.

This was only their second day in Ireland, only three days since his trip to Brighton with Jenny. John was trying to forget the journey to Brighton, and trying to forget the stories of the man on the cassette and of the policeman. He had not told Rachel about any of that last day at work. The stories had frightened him. It had frightened him that the man's story was so similar to his own first meeting with Rachel. He didn't want to talk to Rachel about it. He would not know how to tell her or what to tell her. Anyway, talking to her would make it all seem real. He preferred to think of it as a dream, a dream that he could forget.

He hoped that being in Ireland would make him feel better, would help him forget. This was a place where he had spent many holidays by himself and where he and Rachel had spent their first holiday together. He always felt peaceful here. He hoped that those feelings of peace would come back to him now. Now more than ever he needed to have those feelings of peace.

He stood at the front of the boat and watched the seven dark round mountains of Connemara that rose behind the fishing port they had just left. They were not large mountains, not by world standards, but from the sea they looked high enough. They also looked very attractive, very inviting, very safe. But if the weather changed, and it changed very quickly here, and if the fog and rain came in from the Atlantic, then it became very dangerous. Then, when you could not see your foot in front of you in the thick fog, it became very dangerous. Then you could get lost. Then you could disappear for ever.

The boat was turning now beside the Cliffs of Moher, the black cliffs that rose straight out of the sea to a height of over one hundred metres. John looked up at the cliffs, and felt small. It was difficult to believe that the tiny shapes he could just see at the top were people. They were so small, so far away.

Rachel and he had walked along these cliffs on their first holiday here. They had walked alone at sunset and had danced to the songs he sang in her ear. Then they had walked a little further until they stopped and stood silently. Both were quiet in their own thoughts before a small monument that was placed at the edge of the cliff. They bent down to read what was written on it:

To Sean
We miss you each and every day.
We live for the day when we will all meet again in
a better place.

There was no date on the monument. There was nothing to show how or when Sean had died. There was nothing to show how old he was, or who had left this stone here in his memory, a metre from the edge of the cliff.

John moved closer to the edge to look down into the dark blue-green water that broke into waves far below but Rachel pulled him back sharply by his arm.

'John, don't. Be careful.'

He smiled at her.

'It's OK.'

He then bent down, picked up a small stone and threw it gently over the edge. He tried to follow its fall to the sea but he lost it long before it reached the water and he heard no sound as it hit the water and disappeared for ever into the ocean.

Shouts from people around him on the boat woke John from his memories. He looked around, not sure what was happening. Everyone was shouting. He looked for Rachel and Patrick but they were not standing where they had been. A sudden feeling of sickness rose from his stomach to the back of his mouth as he stared into the sea behind the boat.

He thought he could see something in the water. But the shouts were coming from the side of the boat and, as he ran down the steps, he could see almost everyone on the boat was there. He saw Rachel and Patrick near the side of the boat. Patrick was pointing at something and shouting. His eyes and mouth were wide open. John looked over the side of the boat but could see nothing.

But then, suddenly, something black and grey jumped out of the water and dived in again, and jumped and dived again and then again and he realised it was a dolphin and that the dolphin was swimming beside the boat, racing it.

Another dolphin appeared and the two dolphins now jumped together from the water and then dived back into the cold sea.

'Look Patrick,' he heard Rachel say as he moved behind her, 'the dolphin's mummy has come to make sure he's all right. She looks after him, just like I look after you. See?'

The smaller dolphin swam with them a little longer but the bigger one did not come back and then the small one too swam away from the side of the boat, doing a final jump as if to say goodbye.

'Good sign that,' said a man standing beside John. John was not sure who the man was talking to. 'They look after people at sea, people in danger. A sign of life too, you know, of life even after death,' the man said.

'Really?' asked John, but Patrick was shouting in his ear now about the 'fish' and John had to turn away from the man and listen to Patrick.

He saw the man again when the boat arrived at the island of Inishbofin, but only in the distance as he walked away from the port. John and Rachel waited until everyone else had got off. Then they collected all their bags, full of food and clothes, and got off the boat themselves. By that time the man had already disappeared and they did not see him again as they walked towards the cottage.

The cottage was on the east coast of the island. This was where most of the islanders lived. There were still only ten or twelve cottages here, all looking back towards the mainland of Ireland. There were also two pubs where people went for the nightly music and the Guinness.

*   *   *

John especially loved the west coast, which was wild and empty, where no-one lived and where the winds from the North Atlantic came racing in.

'Next stop, New York,' John said to himself as he stood looking out into the empty sea. It was near the end of their week on the island and he had come for one last long walk alone, from one end of the island to the other. From the north end where the cliffs were high and it was impossible to reach the beach, to the more gentle south where the sheep ate the grass, keeping it as short and tidy as on a golf course.

He loved this place. He had walked now for almost three hours and had seen hundreds of birds carried on the wind, diving into the sea for fish. He had also seen hundreds of sheep that ran away with frightened cries before he even came close to them. He had not seen a single person on his walk. True, he had looked down on to a small, golden beach and had seen two bicycles lying on the sand with two sets of footprints going away from them towards the bottom of the cliff as if two young lovers were looking for a quiet place.

But he had not seen anyone. That was why he now stopped and looked at the person in black who was sitting on the rocks near the sea. John was perhaps two hundred metres away from the person so it was difficult to see if it was a man or a woman. The person was dressed in a black suit and had either very short hair or no hair at all, but from this distance that was all John could see. He, if it was a man, was sitting totally still, looking out to sea but not moving his head, not moving at all. John stood and watched the man and then he too turned towards the sea, in the direction the man was looking. He could see nothing and when he turned back, the man had gone. Disappeared. Nothing surprising in that. There were so many places where he might have gone, hidden from view by the rocks. Maybe the man had noticed John and had decided to look for a place where he would be completely alone. John could understand that. He was looking for the same thing. He just hoped that the man would not come near the pool, *his* pool.

The pool was a rock pool, just a few metres from the ocean's edge. It was filled and refilled every day by the ocean as the waves broke over the rocks. John had found it on a previous visit when he had been on the island by himself. He had been walking for hours when he came to the pool and his feet were hot and tired. He had sat down beside the pool on a rock.

At first he had taken off only his boots and socks and rested his feet in the cool quiet water. It was wonderfully cold and inviting. John then looked around to make sure there was no-one around and then he took off all his clothes and climbed slowly into the pool. He didn't swim much as the pool was small. Instead he lay on his back looking at the few small white clouds racing across the open sky.

Then he turned over on his face for a moment, his eyes open, his mouth closed, his arms hanging below him in the water, not moving, almost as if he were dead. As this thought went through John's head he turned over in the water, afraid that someone might walk past the pool and see him and think he was dead.

Now, as he came to the pool again, he took off his clothes and climbed in, as he had done the first time. Then, as before, he dried himself with his cotton shirt and lay down on some grass near the pool and went to sleep. But this time his sleep would not be so restful.

Chapter 9   *Sleeping by the pool*

He woke in the cottage, although at first he did not know where he was. He lay still for a moment. It was very dark and he could not see much. He knew where he was only by the smells, the smell of the dried earth they burn in the fireplaces in the west of Ireland and the smell of the sheets, fresh from drying outside in the wind. But it was still difficult to see. There were no street lights on the island, no lights from street advertisements, no car lights going past. There was a darkness and a silence that you never get in the town. It was one of the things that John loved about the island.

But as he woke now, he did not feel comfortable. He did not like the darkness of the room where he lay. It made him feel nervous. He felt something was not quite right. Slowly, from the darkness, he began to recognise shapes: the lighter-coloured walls and the dark shapes of the heavy furniture in the cottage – the large wardrobe at the end of the bed where they put their clothes and where they could have put twice as many clothes, the painting on the wall of the two men on the beach pushing their little boat into the high waves of the Atlantic.

As he began to realise where he was he also knew that something was very wrong. The room was quiet. Quieter than it should be. He could hear only the outside noises of the sea and a wind that whispered through the windows of the cottage. There were no noises from inside the cottage. He reached over in the bed towards Rachel, but knew already before his hand touched the cold sheets that she was not there. He sat up in bed and tried to say her name but nothing came out. He tried to shout but nothing came. His breathing was fast and very loud. He pulled the sheets back and threw them off the bed and saw that it was still empty. He got out of bed and ran to the wardrobe and opened it and looked inside it. Then he ran to the window and pulled back the curtains. He looked out into the darkness, pushing his face against the cold wet window and silently called Rachel's name. He could see no-one outside. He turned to the little bed where Patrick lay and tried to scream again as he saw that that bed was empty too.

He ran to the living room, pushing and kicking at the furniture that got in his way. He screamed her name and this time it came out; from the bottom of his stomach the name came and he put his hands to his ears to stop it. It hurt so much to hear her name when she was not there, when she had gone.

He ran to the front door and pulled at it but it did not move. The key was in the lock and he turned it. But it simply turned and turned and the lock did not move. He ran back to the bedroom and stopped suddenly as he saw that the wardrobe door was opening. It opened slowly and someone stepped out. It was someone in black. The white of the face was the only light in the room. It was impossible to see if it was a man or a woman. It was carrying something. It spoke. The voice was the man's from the boat.

'The baby's fine. Don't worry.' And John saw that the man was holding Patrick.

John tried to speak but his mouth was dry and he could not produce any words but he heard the questions as if someone else was asking them.

'What are you . . . who are you? What are you doing with my son? Where is . . . ?'

'The boy is fine,' the man said. 'It's all right. He'll be OK now. They don't really die, you know, they come back. The little ones who go before their time. They come back from the other side. They always come back to us. They always come back.'

'What! What are you talking about? What do you mean, come back? What other side? What are you talking about? You mean death? My son is fine. He's not dead! Are you mad? And . . .' John looked around the room again. 'And . . . where is my wife? What have you done to my wife?'

John was trying to look into the man's face but it was still difficult to see anything. He noticed that the man's hair was very short but that was all he could see. The man spoke again. He spoke with a voice that was gentle and soft.

'Her work is done now. She can go back to the other side. You can let her go now. She has done very well. Look at the boy, the boy is fine. A lovely child.'

John looked at Patrick asleep in the man's arms and reached out to take him but as he put out his arms he felt himself start to fall backwards. Slowly at first, very slowly. The man was still speaking. His mouth formed the words but John could no longer hear the words. And now John felt as if he was falling faster and faster. But the man still stood there and did not seem any further away. With his whole body John knew that he was falling, even though nothing around him moved. He reached out again with his arms. The man too was reaching out his hand. Although John was still falling the hand came closer and closer, and finally it touched the side of his face. Everything stopped, then suddenly everything went dark.

Chapter 10   *Dreams untold, dreams told*

Rachel was bending over John, touching his face. He opened his eyes. He could see her mouth moving but he could hear nothing and then slowly her words came to him.

'John? John? Are you OK? I was going crazy with worry. You were gone for hours. What happened? You look terrible. I was frightened. I thought something had happened to you. Are you OK? What happened? John, speak to me!'

His throat was very dry and he found it difficult to say anything, but finally he managed to speak.

'Where am I? Where's Patrick?'

He sat up and looked around him. He was still beside the pool. Slowly he began to remember where he was. The sun was much lower in the sky now than when he had fallen asleep.

'I fell asleep. I had a dream. It was terrible. A terrible dream, a nightmare. It was awful. I thought you'd gone away. I thought you'd left me. I couldn't find you. I looked everywhere. It was awful. Oh God, it was awful. And the man had Patrick. Patrick! Where is he? Where's Patrick?'

'He's fine. He's fine, my love. Mrs Reagan is looking after him.'

'Mrs Reagan?'

'Yes, you know, the woman from the pub. He's fine. He's fine.' She pulled him close to her and held him tight. She pushed her face against his hair and held him. She held him as he cried. He cried as she had never seen him cry before.

'I thought you'd gone,' he said. 'I thought you'd gone.'

He repeated the words over and over again between his tears.

She held him tightly for a long time until slowly his tears stopped, although his whole body was still shaking. And then slowly she helped him to his feet and they began to walk away from the pool. They walked towards the path that led to the other side of the island and back to the cottages.

They didn't speak as they walked but she could feel the strength slowly returning to his body. She was no longer helping him to walk but was just holding his arm with her hand. She needed to hold him now as much as he needed to be held by her. As they came towards the cottages and the first pub they turned to each other.

'I thought I'd lost you.'

'I thought I'd lost you.'

They spoke the words together. Both of them. The same words at the same moment. And then they fell into each other's arms and held each other, and this time they were both crying. They stood like that for some time. They stood still like the people in a painting that hung in one of the local pubs. A painting of a man and a woman holding each other and crying, as if one of them was going away for a long time, for ever perhaps.

This island had seen many goodbyes like this as the men had left to find work in England or America. They made their promises to return soon or to send money so that the women could join them. Sometimes the money arrived, sometimes not even a letter arrived.

Sometimes the man came back.

'I'm OK now, honestly,' John said as Rachel pulled back from him a little and looked up into his face questioningly. 'Really,' he continued, 'it was a dream. It was a terrible dream but it was just a dream. I'm OK. I'm OK. I think maybe I was more tired than I thought I was. It was only a dream. I'm OK. Really, I'm OK.'

*　　*　　*

They returned to the pub and found Patrick playing happily with Mrs Reagan.

'Ah, he's a lovely boy! He's a darling. I could keep him for myself. It's a pleasure to look after him. It really is. You know, next time you come you must stay here at the pub and I can look after him for you.'

'Have you got a room?' John asked.

'Sure you know we have rooms, John.'

'No, I mean, do you have a free room now? For this coming week?'

'John? We're going back tomorrow,' Rachel reminded him.

'I know, but I think maybe I need a longer rest. I don't want to go back just yet. I could phone the office and tell them I'm taking another week's holiday. What do you think? And look at Patrick. He's enjoying this so much. He's not going to get the chance to see much sand or sea in London, is he? And he's so safe here, isn't he? No traffic, nothing. Come on, what do you say? Shall we stay?'

'But after your . . . after that . . . are you sure you want to stay after . . . ?'

'It was a dream, Rachel, it was a horrible dream but it was only a dream. I've had a few bad dreams recently but that was only a dream, nothing else. I dreamt I had lost you . . .' His voice almost broke again. He took a deep breath and then he finished his thought. 'And now I just want to stay here for another week and have some time with you. I don't want to go back to work just yet.'

*   *   *

And so they stayed a second week on the island, but not in the cottage. They moved to the pub, to a room above the bar. It was certainly more noisy, especially at nights. The island pubs seemed to close when they wanted and they never wanted to until three o'clock in the morning. But Patrick slept through it all and John preferred the noise to the silence now. He and Rachel often joined the crowd downstairs in the pub for the singing and the 'crack', as the Irish call good conversation, and Mrs Reagan was always happy to look after Patrick.

'I'd rather look after this darling boy than listen to these old fools talking,' she had said looking at her husband and his brother who also worked in the pub, and they had all laughed.

But after the pub closed John still found it difficult to go to sleep and he hated it if he woke up in the darkness. It reminded him too much of his dream. When he did go to bed he lay close to Rachel rather than facing away from her, as he usually did when they slept together. He liked to be close enough to her to feel her breathing.

They had not talked any more about his nightmare. John did not want to. He wanted to forget about it. He wanted especially to forget what the man in black had said

63

about Patrick and about Rachel. He wanted to forget this dream as he was already trying to forget the story of the hitch-hiker in white. He wanted to forget all that. He just wanted to hold on to his wife. He realised that for the first time in their marriage there were things that he was not telling Rachel. He did not like it but he did not want to talk about these things.

He lay beside Rachel, his hand resting on her stomach, feeling it rise and fall with her sleeping breath. He didn't want to let go of her. He was almost afraid to fall asleep.

As the week went on, however, he began to relax and stopped looking nervously over his shoulder every time the pub door opened. But he didn't go on any more long walks by himself. They walked mainly down to the nearby beach where Patrick was discovering the pleasure of sand. It was a full-time job for John to keep the sand out of Patrick's mouth, hair, eyes and other parts of the body. He enjoyed having the time to spend with his son and he promised himself that he would spend more time with Patrick in the future and less time at work.

On the last night he and Rachel went together for a walk, leaving Patrick with Mrs Reagan. It was the first time they had been out together without Patrick on this holiday. They walked to the end of the island where a large fishing boat had washed up on the rocks fifteen years before. It was an amazing sight. This large boat was sitting on the rocks fifty metres from the sea. It had sat in the same place since it had been caught in a storm and the waves had thrown it onto the rocks.

'It's amazing, isn't it? It's like a big toy. Patrick would love this,' said John walking around the boat and looking up at it. 'They didn't have the money to get it moved back to the sea, so they just left it here. Amazing.'

He was still looking up at the boat when Rachel spoke softly behind him.

'I want to tell you about my dream. About the dream *I* had before Patrick's birthday. Remember?'

John nodded.

'I can tell you about it now. Now that we're here and now that his birthday is over. Now I feel he's safe, you know.'

'Are you sure?'

'Yes. I want to. It was terrible. Like your dream, but I want to talk about it now.'

She sat down and John sat beside her, their backs against the side of the boat and she began.

'I had the dream three or four times. I dreamt I was with a child, but it wasn't Patrick. He was very like Patrick, but it wasn't him. And we were getting ready for his birthday party. He was sitting behind me on the floor and was playing with a toy car and making noises, making car noises. And I felt really happy. I had this lovely warm feeling inside, and I knew I had never been happier, and I was singing to myself and smiling . . . and . . .'

John put his arm around Rachel and she smiled at him and nodded but the smile did not come easily this time.

'And then,' she continued, 'then it all changed. Suddenly I felt something was wrong and I wanted to turn round and look at him but I couldn't . . . I couldn't turn round. I couldn't even turn my head to look at him. And then I realised that the noises I was hearing were not his car noises any more. They were not the car noises he was making.

They were real car noises and it was suddenly dark and I wasn't in the house and I was . . . I don't know where I was. And then the car noises got louder and louder and there was a scream and a crash and the world seemed to be turning over and over and I couldn't see the baby and . . . And then I woke up. I had this same dream again and again and again, and I was getting really frightened. I was afraid something was going to happen to Patrick. I don't know what. But I was afraid of cars, I was afraid to be near them. I was afraid something was going to happen to Patrick before his birthday. I was sure something bad was going to happen before his birthday. It was awful. But it's OK now. He's safe. We're all safe, aren't we? And everything's fine now, isn't it? It was just a dream, wasn't it? Just like yours was a dream. My dream didn't mean anything. And yours didn't mean anything either. Did it?'

John kept his arms around Rachel as she pushed her face against his chest. He held her in his arms.

'It's all right now,' he said.

Rachel couldn't see his face, couldn't see the expression on his face. His face had turned white again and he looked frightened. He was remembering the policeman's story of the car accident and of the baby that had died. He was remembering what the man in black had said about a baby 'coming back from the other side'. He was remembering the man's story of the hitch-hiker on the road from Brighton. And now Rachel's dream about a baby in a car accident!

'It's all right now,' he said again. 'It's all right.'

But John wasn't sure that he believed what he was saying. He wasn't sure he believed his own words.

Chapter 11   *Stop it! Stop it!*

John stood in their bedroom at home. It was Sunday evening. They had returned from Ireland the day before and now John was getting ready for work the next day. He always got his clothes ready the night before. It gave him an extra few minutes in bed the next morning. An extra few minutes to lie close to Rachel in the warmth before he had to get up and go to work. He took his dark blue jacket out of the wardrobe. He held it against himself and stood in front of the mirror. It was a jacket he often wore to work. He looked at himself. He looked relaxed and sun-tanned after their two-week holiday.

But he did not feel relaxed. He'd felt relaxed for a while in the middle of the holiday, but Rachel's dream had brought back all his fears. There were so many questions he could not answer about the dreams and the stories of the policeman and the man on the cassette. They were questions he did not even want to think about. But he could not forget them.

He picked up his wallet from the table beside the bed and put it into his jacket pocket. There was something already in his pocket. A box. It felt like a cigarette packet but that wasn't possible. He had stopped smoking over ten years before. But now he almost hoped it was a packet of cigarettes. Now he felt he wanted a cigarette. Now he felt he needed a cigarette. He took the thing out of his pocket and looked at it. It was an audio cassette box. He opened it. There was a cassette inside. Nothing was written on the cassette and, for a moment, he wondered what it was and then he remembered.

The last time he had worn this jacket was his last day at work. The day Jenny and he had driven down to Brighton. And this was the cassette they had listened to in his office. The cassette from the radio station with the story of the lady in white. He must have put it in his pocket when they left his office that Friday.

John stood and looked at the cassette in his hand and all the feelings he'd had that day came back to him now. His mouth was suddenly very dry and his stomach seemed to drop to his feet.

'John, dinner's ready. Are you coming down?' It was Rachel calling from downstairs.

'I'm coming,' he answered.

He looked at the cassette in his hand. He put it down on the table beside the bed but then picked it up again immediately. He didn't want Rachel to find it. Instead he put it back in his pocket and went downstairs. He would do something with it later.

They had dinner together. John was very quiet while they ate but this did not surprise Rachel. He was often like this at the end of a holiday. He enjoyed his work but he found it difficult to go back to it after a holiday. The last night after a holiday was usually difficult for him, so she did not say anything about his silence.

They went to bed early and Rachel fell asleep quickly, as she always did. She always slept well, but she woke up immediately if Patrick made any noise at all. Tonight Patrick was sleeping very quietly.

John, however, could not sleep. Seeing the cassette again had brought back the whole story of the lady in white. He could almost hear the man's voice in his head telling the story, telling the man's story, telling John's story. Rachel lay quietly beside him. John did not reach out to touch her as he normally did when he woke in the middle of the night. Pictures filled his head like a film playing too fast, like one film mixed up with another. Pictures of Rachel dressed in white on the cliffs in Ireland mixed with words from the story about the hitch-hiker. Pictures of Rachel standing on a lonely road near Brighton mixed with pictures and noises of cars crashing. Pictures of their bedroom in Ireland and the words of a man dressed in black. Words about Patrick 'coming back from the other side' and 'her work is done. She can go back to the other side now'.

John was becoming hotter and hotter as he lay in bed. His thoughts jumped from place to place, but he sat up immediately and went cold when he heard the scream.

He sat in bed listening. Rachel did not move. He heard nothing, only Rachel's quiet breathing. He went quickly to Patrick's room and looked down at the child's bed. Patrick was also sleeping quietly. He looked out of the window. There was no-one. There had been no scream that anyone else could hear. The scream, like the pictures, was all in his head. He stood watching Patrick. Patrick was quiet, but was he safe? Was Rachel safe? He walked slowly to the wardrobe and opened the door as he had done in his dream. He looked through the clothes. He did not know what or who he was looking for. There were clothes, only clothes.

John went into the next bedroom and sat on the bed there with his head in his hands and closed his eyes and tried to see nothing.

'What is going on here? What is happening to me? What is happening to me? Am I going mad? What does this all mean? Oh God, help me, help me. Please help me, I don't understand any of this.'

He sat with his head in his hands and cried softly to himself.

He must have slept a few hours because when he opened his eyes again it was already light. He washed and dressed without waking Rachel. He left the house without waking her. He did not touch her or kiss her goodbye, as he usually did. He just got into his car and drove off.

Slowly, as he drove, his thoughts began to become calmer. In the daylight things seemed different. The night before began to seem like another bad dream. His worst fears and worries always came in the middle of the night. In the morning he looked back and could not believe how he had felt, what he had done in the night. 'There is an explanation to all of this,' he thought.

He began to think of work and his mood began to improve. It was a beautiful morning and John enjoyed driving – the beauty of the morning was helping to push away the dark thoughts of his sleepless night. He began to relax and to look forward to getting back to work. He turned on the cassette player in the car and pushed the play button. It was a cassette with some of his favourite Irish songs. The song that was playing was painfully sad.

Hillhall, Ireland
Eighteen ninety
My dear and loving son, John

I'm sorry to bring you
The very sad news
That your dear old mother
Has passed on
We buried her down by
The river in Moira
Beside your young brother Tom

John started to cry, gently. He thought of his own mother who had died four years before. Before he had met Rachel. He could see his mother's face in front of him. He could see the small church where they had held the funeral service for her. He began to cry now as he had cried when his mother had died. He tried to dry his eyes with the back of his hand as he continued to look at the road ahead of him.

As he dried his eyes the music disappeared and John heard the voice of the man instead, telling the story of the hitch-hiker, of the lady in white. John looked at the cassette player. A man's voice was coming from it now. It was the man's voice from the radio programme.

I just wanted to get her out of the car. I said, 'We'll soon be there,' but she didn't answer. Then suddenly, as I was getting close to a bend in the road, she started to scream. I went cold inside . . .

John hit the stop button on the cassette player but the voice continued.

. . . and my stomach jumped and she was screaming, 'Oh

God, we're losing control, we're losing control, watch out, watch out, oh my God!'

John pressed a button on the cassette player and the cassette jumped out, but the voice continued. John started shouting to cover the sound of the other voice. He did not want to hear this story again.

'Stop it, stop it. I don't want to hear this. Do you hear me! Stop it. Stop it. I've had enough of this!' John shouted and hit the cassette player with his left hand. The tears filled John's eyes. The voice continued.

. . . and she was looking at me. She was looking at me . . . it's difficult to describe the look but . . . I don't know what it was, it was like she was trying to see what kind of person I was. It was, I don't know, it was almost sexy and yet uncertain, as if she didn't know if she could trust me or not. I mean, after the tears and everything, it made me feel, sort of excited and nervous at the same time. And a bit uncomfortable.

John could hardly see the road in front of him.

'Stop it! Stop it! Stop it!' he shouted and hit blindly at the cassette player with his left hand. His whole body was shaking now and he was shouting non-stop.

'Stop it! Stop it! Stop it! Stop it! I don't want to hear this again. This is not about me. Do you understand? This is nothing to do with me. This is not my story. Stop it, stop it! Leave me alone. Please. Please leave us alone!'

Behind him a car was blowing its horn and flashing its lights. A car coming towards John was also flashing its lights. John hardly noticed through his tears. And then suddenly he realised that the voice had stopped. He also realised that his car was going wildly from one side of the road to the other. He heard for the first time the horn of the car behind him and saw the flashing lights of the cars coming towards him.

He pulled his car over to the side of the road and stopped. The car that had been travelling behind drove past. The driver turned to look at John and pointed to his head with his fingers as if to say, 'Are you mad?'

John didn't notice him. As his car had come to a stop he put his head in his hands and started to cry violently.

Chapter 12   *Don't look back*

John sat for some time in his car and then drove to work. He sat in his office but he could not think about work. The success of his television programmes seemed empty now. He got back into his car and drove around London for hours. Once or twice he saw road signs for Brighton. He stopped his car and looked at the signs. He thought about driving back to the village. But it was getting dark and he decided to go home instead.

He was not looking forward to going home. When he arrived home dinner was ready. John was quiet as they ate.

'Are you OK, John? You're very quiet. Is anything the matter? Did something happen at the office?'

'I'm fine,' he said. 'You know I always find it difficult going back to work.'

'Are you worried about something? You've been so quiet since that last day in Ireland. If there was something wrong you would tell me, wouldn't you? John? You would tell me?'

'Yes, of course. But I'm fine. I'm fine. It's just going back to work, you know.'

He stood up and walked around the table towards her. She thought he was going to kiss her, but instead he just put his hand on her shoulder.

'I'm fine. Really.'

Rachel went to bed early but John stayed up.

'There's a programme on TV I want to see,' he said.

When he did go to bed later he couldn't get to sleep. He was almost afraid to go to sleep. Afraid of what he might dream. And he didn't feel comfortable lying beside Rachel. He went to the next room again and slept a little. At breakfast Rachel asked him again what the matter was. They had never slept in separate beds before in this house. But John only said that he was thinking about work and could not sleep. That it was nothing important. That there was nothing wrong.

They both knew, for the first time, that there was something unspoken between them. But John could not say more. How could he tell her about the strange thoughts that raced through his head as he lay in the middle of the night in the darkness?

'I'll be working late this evening,' he said. 'I did almost no work yesterday. You know what it's like at work on the first day after a holiday. I'll be back late. Don't make dinner for me.'

John got into his car and drove off but he didn't go to work. He drove around for hours again and then finally he took the road for Brighton and went back to the village where he had first met Rachel and where the three men had met the hitch-hiker.

He sat there in his car for hours and then went home. But the next night he came back to the village again, and then, on the third night, he was back again, sitting in his car at the exact place where he had first met Rachel.

On the first night he had come here he had seen nothing. But on the second night something appeared suddenly in the rear view mirror of his car. John's hair stood on end. He heard footsteps beside the car but he continued to look straight ahead. Then the footsteps moved on and he heard a dog. He relaxed as a man walked past with the dog, but then the man stopped. He looked back towards the car, bending down a little as he tried to look inside. John waved but the man was obviously wondering who was sitting here alone in a car late at night. The man walked on but returned a few minutes later on the other side of the road. Then the man started to cross the road and walk towards the car. John started the engine quickly and drove off. He did not want to explain to the man what he was doing. He had no explanation that would make any sense. He did not really know why he had to come back again.

And now John sat in his car in the village for the third night. It was a wet night and the car, which had been warm after his journey, was now getting very cold. The inside of the car windows was wet from his breath and it was getting difficult to see anything clearly through them. He cleaned the windows with the arm of his jacket. There was not much to see. The road that went up the hill in front of him was empty and dark. There were no street lights in front of him and the ones behind him from the village did not come this far. The road was empty in both directions. He had been sitting here for half an hour already and only two or three cars had passed. He cleaned the rear view mirror again and turned on the heater in the back window. The window slowly began to clear and he could see out. He could see the road behind more clearly now in the mirror. A few lights from some of the houses helped the street lights. He could see the first house behind him quite clearly. The two front windows were lit up and he thought he could see someone sitting inside but maybe it was just a piece of furniture. An armchair perhaps. The other houses were only dark shapes behind him, nothing more. He shook with the cold and he asked himself what he was doing here, why he had come back to the village again and again.

He had been here for three nights already. No-one had come. No lady in white. Is that who he expected? Did he think she came here every night, this mysterious hitch-hiker? And if she did come, if she did come tonight, what then? Well, then he would know, wouldn't he? Then, one way or another he would know. Either it would be as Jenny had said, a woman looking for her memory, or . . . Who else could it be? Rachel? Did he really think it could be Rachel? Did he really think that this lady in white was Rachel?

And if this lady in white didn't come? If no-one came, as no-one had come the first night, and no-one had come the second night. What then? Would he continue to drive half-way to Brighton from London, park here and wait, wait until another villager saw him and called the police. Wait here for how many nights? And if no-one ever came, what would that mean? This was madness. This was completely mad. This was not helping him get back to a normal life. This would destroy him, this would . . .

There was a flash of white in the rear mirror. He thought at first it was a light and he looked again deep into the mirror but the white was still there. The white of a dress. A woman in white. A woman in white was standing just behind the car, not moving. He could see only part of her body. He could not see her legs, he could not see her head, or face. Because of where she was standing he could only see part of her in the rear-view mirror. He did not want to turn around and look at her. He was afraid. He looked into the side mirror and could see a little more. Yes, a woman. It was definitely a woman. But he could still not see the head, nor the face. He felt even colder inside now. His stomach suddenly felt very empty. His hands felt as if they were stuck to the steering wheel. He could not move and she did not move. And then suddenly she took a step forward and John watched her disappear from the rear-view mirror. He looked at the side mirror as she took another step forward.

'Oh God, what is going on?' he whispered to himself.

The woman moved forward and then stopped beside the car, beside the passenger door. John turned and looked. The dress was close to the window now and he heard a noise as her hand reached down for the handle of the door. The handle moved, but the door was locked and John did not move to open it. Her hand came up and rested on the window. Her right hand. He looked at her hand. There were no rings on her long sun-tanned fingers. She lifted one finger as if to knock on the window or maybe to write something on the wet glass and then the hand moved away and she also moved back from the car. She moved slowly so more of her body could be seen through the window. She stepped back a little more, and he could see more and then she took another step and John could see her neck and then . . .

John drove almost a kilometre without turning the car lights on. He had started the engine and, as the woman had stepped back, the car had jumped forward and he had looked straight ahead and was gone, five hundred metres down the road even before he knew what he was doing.

He didn't look back. He wasn't going to look back. He was not going to look back along this road and he was not going to look back on anything that had happened over the last month or so. He remembered, for the last time he told himself, the dream he'd had on the island. He didn't want to lose his wife. He wasn't going to lose his wife. He was certainly not going to lose her as a result of the madness his own mind had been making over the last few weeks.

He drove on. There was no other traffic on the road and he drove faster than was safe on such a dark, wet night. It seemed as dark as it had been in the cottage in Ireland. As dark as it had been in his dream.

He had driven almost thirty kilometres from the village in less than twenty minutes when he noticed something in his rear view mirror. There seemed to be a light coming from the back seat of the car. He slowed down and turned around to look at the back seat.

His mobile phone was lying on the seat and the light was coming from it. The phone. He could phone Rachel. She would be at home. He thought again of the lady in white whose face he hadn't wanted to see. That had been twenty minutes ago. That woman had not been Rachel. Rachel was at home. He could phone her now and she would answer. He stopped the car at the side of the road and picked up the phone.

He sat for a minute looking at it. It would take him another thirty minutes to drive home, even driving as fast as he was. No-one could have driven from the village to their house and arrived there by now. It was impossible. He could phone Rachel now and she would be at home and he would know that the lady in white was someone else. And still he could only sit and look at the phone and his fears returned.

And then he called his home number. The phone rang. No-one answered. It continued to ring and then he heard a voice. It was his own voice on the answer machine.

'I'm sorry that Rachel and John are not here to take your call at the moment but if you would like to . . .'

His eyes filled with tears again and he could hardly breath and then suddenly the message stopped and he could hear Rachel's voice.

'Hello . . .' Her voice was sleepy.

'Rachel?'

'John? Where are you? Are you all right? I was sleeping when the phone rang.'

'I'm fine, my love. I'm on my way home now. I'll be there in about half an hour. Will you wait up for me?

'Of course I will.'

'Rachel?'

'Yes.'

'I love you.'

'I love you too, John. Come home soon.'

'I will . . . I will.'

He started the car for the journey home and he would not look back until he got there.